Swear
Down

Swear
Down

Nick Moss

STACK
BOOKS

Smokestack Books
1 Lake Terrace, Grewelthorpe,
Ripon HG4 3BU
e-mail: info@smokestack-books.co.uk
www.smokestack-books.co.uk

ISBN 9781838198886

Smokestack Books
is represented by
Inpress Ltd

Contents

Prisoner Information Notice   11
Can the Seas Know Shame?   13
The Magic Bus   14
Living Ghosts   15
Hauntings   16
C Wing Symphony   18
HMP Brixton Chapel   20
Psi 30/2013   23
Racaille   24
96 Tears   25
Lying   26
Norman   27
Paddy   29
Prison Works   31
Rats in a Barrel   33
Talking Yourself into a Hole   34
A Harlesden Crackhead Speaks of John Coltrane   35
A Rancid Poetry   36
Abdi's Blue Guitar   38
Acrostic   39
Another Postcode Warrior Gone Straight on the Numbers   40
Candy Flip   44
Citizens of Nowhere   46
Comedians   48
Eviction Day   49
Games   51
My Man Courtney Was Shit at Maths   52
Never Again?   53
Nights   55
No Cream, No Crystal   56
Angie   57
On Lucian Freud's *Two Irishmen in W11*   58
Prison Pallor   59
Redemption   60
Rescue   62

Mates	64
Spaces	65
Steps	66
Swear Down	67
The Beautiful Boys and Girls	69
The Best of Society	71
The Exact Reverse is True	72
The Victors are Always Victors	74
To Hell with Property	75
Top Shotta	76
Life Sentence	77
William Burroughs on Brownlow Hill	78
Autumnal	79
The Ronnie Spector of Shiel Road	80
Mystery Trains	82
In Memoriam	83
Drug War Poems	84
Hawks	86
Alive	87
I Used to be Somebody Else	88

Prisoner Information Notice

'Due to the increase in demand for spaces, the monthly "double visit sessions" will finish on 30th March 2015.'

Paroxetine
Pregabs
Subotex

'It is your responsibility to make sure that you retain your Enhanced status as any downgrade prior to a Sunday visit will be cancelled up to 48 hours in advance.'

Lofepramine
Thorazine
Citalopram

'Using illicit drugs is damaging to your health and affects your thinking skills'.

Melleril
Prozac
Zopiclone

'If any employed prisoner is suspected of being under the influence of any illicit substances, they will be removed from their work area and will face immediate dismissal.'

Spice
Smack
Skunk

'There are no transfers to other open prisons scheduled and it is unlikely that there will be any in the near future.'

Setraline
Venlafaxine
Seroxat

'I would encourage you to work towards home leave and ROTL opportunities to maximise the time you get to spend with family and friends.'

Can the Seas Know Shame?

Can the seas know shame?
All those desperate, now dead
thrown up on Europe's shores.
The tide spits up a plastic bead,
the dull eye from some child's toy.

Hundreds daring every day.
The shame is ours,
who always look away.

The Magic Bus

It doesn't quite rate with
Kissinger winning the Nobel Peace Prize,
but it catches in the throat
that the Serco bus to Belmarsh
has rose-tinted plexiglass
on its windows.

Living Ghosts

Do we fall from your minds
as we drop from view,
as the court moves on
to its next part-heard case?

As we descend the stairs
to social death
do we lose forever
all that went before?

We are living ghosts.
Let us lie with you
in your dreams,
that we might cheat this
death-in-life.
if only 'til you wake,
and we are lost once more.

Hauntings

It's a week since Peter went home,
feels like a life ago.
It happens all the time,
one day here,
in all our lives.
the next day gone.
Time up or shipped out.
Either way
another voice just echoing now
on the wing.

We slip in and out of each other's lives,
walk the landings, revenants
carrying our souls in plastic sacks.
We haunt each other for a while,
then flash away,
like shadows do
when the sun hits the yard.

Yesterday we talked
behind a metal door
of all the fears of home,
of life; of kids not seen for 10 plus years;
adrenaline kicks and white lines crossed
and snorted; anticipation of cold beers
and family curses
Now you're out again,
hoping for notoriety,
but knowing you just face shame.

Carrying our souls in plastic sacks,
we haunt each other for a while,
then flash away
like shadows do
when the sun hits the yard

Jail-pale ghosts.
No more real to each other here
than we are to our lives at home.

C Wing Symphony

Dee can't cope with silence,
sub-bass soundtrack whenever he's on the wing.

Two hundred and sixty rotting trainers
beating on three flights of metal stairs.

The skeleton choir singing
'Got any burn?'
'Got any burn?'
'Got any burn?'

A random shouting of names
calling us to heel.
Resounding, resounding, denouncing.
Making sure we know our place here.
The warehoused numbers
on the wing.

The skeleton choir singing
'Got that thing for me?'
'Got that thing for me?'
'Sort you from my next canteen.'

'Freeflow
Freeflow
Freeflow'
But we've never been less free.

P sprawled across two chairs
like he's at the beach.
Cell door open, blasting Sizzla
while the pool balls crack.
A grudging, mumbled 'Shot, mate'
then another wave of bass,
P using bashment
to batter down the walls.

The skeleton choir singing
'Come see me later'
'Come see me later'
'Had my visit, got that rice.'

Freedom songs.
For the not-yet free.

HMP Brixton Chapel

We only went along to support Rio.
Laughing and jostling,
flaunting our non-belief.

The chapel was a spice market,
an assembly of the hollow cheeked
with lightning hands.

Full also of strangers,
come to show their faith
in their idea of God, for sure,
but just as much
a belief in us
we couldn't share.

Rio was preaching
and we pretended not to care,
yet were struck by
how strong he stood,
talking of things
we never mention here,
of fear, and how it might be overcome.

And a priest who told us
that everyone fails,
that failing is what defines us,
failure and forgiveness.

And still those strangers,
watching us waste their time
with our clowning and our dealing
and our exhibition of disrespect.

Then a reading from Matthew,
the sniggers and grunts
at 'For the pagans run
After all these things'
and how the bravado
drained from us all silently
at 'Each day has enough trouble of its own.'

How all of you, though strangers,
greeted us, thanked us,
wished us well,
your presence
a demonstration of your faith
in us, however broken, debased, deluded
we might be.

Refusing, then, to be just strangers,
coming through the gate,
communing with us,
Lifers, IPPs, banged up, cast away.

'For my yoke is easy and my burden light.'
And maybe, for a while,
that's how we felt.
Not unburdened, but less crushed, less down-pressed,
just from the fact
of your coming to us,
giving of your time to us,
strangers to you
and to ourselves.

Telling us our failings
were no worse than yours,
that potential, unrealised,
was not lost, but stored,
latent, the yet-to-come
for those of us
'who are weary and burdened'
rotting here.

We only went along to support Rio,
laughing and jostling
and of a sudden
given rest.

PSI 30/2013

They're burning the books in the library
to ensure compliance with PSI 30/2013

The heating's been off for 2 weeks now.
We pile up extra bedding,
shiver as our balls shrink.

The science of Good Order and Discipline
freeze the mind
and the ass will follow.

If it gets any colder on the wing,
we'll start burning the books here ourselves,
warmed by the flames,
Watching daytime tv

In full compliance with PSI 30/2013

Racaille

My Nigerian cell mate just debated
the interpretation of a verse from Deuteronomy
with the Muslim convert next door.

A kid from New Cross
on a GBH charge
tells me about the fantasy novel
he's written in rhyming verse.

The pool table scrum
is raucous with debate.
Are peace and justice
objects of prayer
or spoils of war?

The spur is a cross between
theological college and philosophy class.
Nietzsche or Christ?
Resurrection or revolution?

A couple of us to the side
sharing a battered James Connolly biography.

We're banged up on basic
three to a cell
can't shit in private.
Racaille.

96 Tears

David Duckenfield has PTSD.
Like Paddy Hill fitted up, screaming at 3am,
flashbacks of beatings and guns to the head?
Like the families of the 96 raging, as the lies cohere
with tabloid complicity, into lifetimes of grief?
David Duckenfield crying 96 crocodile tears
in a witness box.

David Duckenfield has PTSD.
Not guilt, not shame
but PTSD.
Perpetrator as victim
self-serving confessor.
The man who turned Hillsborough
into a death-pit.

David Duckenfield has PTSD.
By happy coincidence
some prisons now offer
Eye Movement Desensitisation and Reprocessing
Lucky David Duckenfield.

Come join us David Duckenfield

Lying

I can't write that they took me away from you.
The blame is mine, the 'they' a lie,
lying here so far from you,
knowing that the best of me is due to you.
Lying together, hearing the foxes bark.
Beyond the razor wire there's barking still
but I'm removed from you,
can't hear you breathe,
can't feel the heat of you.
Hard-felt but simply said – missing you.
I want to say I love you and be truthful and exact
toil for once at truthfulness, as proof of love to you.
I want to hear the foxes bark again,
lying next to you.

Norman

First hand I shook on the wing was yours.
You checked on every new arrival.
Made sure we knew how it all worked here.
Or didn't.

Your endless supply of rotten jokes
At your own expense
(A black Millwall supporter – what else could you expect?)

Always concerned for
the youngers on the wing.
Tried to teach us all
patience, that negotiation
could be an art of war.

You walked the landings
like a parish.
Times when I worried
that you preached defeat.

Remembering when you told us
that if you could change one thing in the world
you'd change nothing,
that change and seeking change only ever
made things worse.

I wondered how many kickings
you'd had to take
to make you think like that.
Wanted to score one small victory here
to show you
things could still be otherwise.

It'll be me soon.
Suddenly
thrown into Being again.
See you on the outside
and I'll try to convince you
that just because we're back 'pon road
doesn't make us free.

Paddy

Fragments of half-remembered rebel songs.
Collapsed veins and yellowed skin.
Longing for the days of
the 'RA on the wing,
and you
vicarious
behind the wire.

The days when you first reached London,
full of love and crack and E.
Six month stretches
in Wandsworth and the Scrubs
but still the rebel,
halfway between Bobby Sands
and Elvis.

Now it's a four-year stint,
a cup of the green every morning,
spice at the weekends.
No visits.
A letter and a postal order
once in a while.

A sweet voice for the singing,
shite skin and life-bleared eyes,
rattling round the wing,
on the cadge
for coffee, burn, sugar.

Wondering where that first love went,
after Holloway
She never came home.
Dead, married, working for probation now,
for all you know.

People like us,
if we have dreams,
the dreams end up in shop doorways
under cardboard,
getting pissed on by strangers.
And our legacy's just shite skin,
self-sabotage and life-bleared eyes.

Singing and rattling round the wings,
hoping a cracked-voiced chorus
of the Wolfetones
will bring down the walls.

Prison Works

'Guilt is always beyond doubt.'
Franz Kafka *In the Penal Colony* (1919)

Staff shortages
so more bang-up
nothing to do
but watch daytime tv

A voiceover tells us
that people like us
are greedy
sticky fingered
drug-addicted
meter-rigging.
A sub-class of shoplifters,
even though what's stolen
is mostly
nappies and formula.

A man in an expensive blue suit
shouts
cheered on by his studio audience.
He tells us
we are 'useless
take no responsibility
blame everybody else.
We should be on our knees
apologising, begging,
but we make no effort
have it easy.
It's all about us.'

The audience applauds.
On set a kid with acne
and a crack habit
weeps.

Suitably degraded, we wait for unlock
And the lunchtime queue.

This is called rehabilitation.

Rats in a Barrel

These are the words that we hide behind:

Real Gs   real niggaz   gangstaz
True talk   real killaz   fuck a pagan
Green paper   stackin'   hustle
Cookin'   cut-up bag   cane
Food   cake   flake
Spice   molly   base   brick
Buss lead   spray
Semi-matic   Uzi   AK   Mac 9
Hit it   drill it   flip it   make it swallow
Bitch   ho   pussy   cunt   gash   sket

Rats in a barrel scratching and crawling for the crumbs we're thrown.

These are the words that we hide behind

No longer making history, we just make moments in time.

Talking Yourself into a Hole

You're talking yourself into a hole.
You're three'd up and shit-scared and bragging
to fill the quiet when your pad mates stop talking,
but you're talking yourself into a hole.

I can hear you; I'm next door
the cell windows are open.
You're full of 'redrum' bravado
but you've confessed twice in the last hour
told us all what the feds don't know,
but you're talking yourself into a hole.

You're 19. You look about 12.
Your lips tremble sometimes and your hands shake.
You don't know your cell mates. You don't know me.
You keep talking yourself into a hole.

And when they serve a new witness statement,
and it comes from the bunk above your head,
and you cry when you're lifed off,
I warned you – you talked yourself into a hole.

A Harlesden Crackhead Speaks of John Coltrane

after Lorna Goodison's 'Town Drunk Recites Omar Khayyam'

Hair matted,
he sways in the road,
asking for a likkle change
from the cars at traffic lights.

Catch him on a good day
he'll tell you he played sax
in Gregory Isaacs' UK backing band,
says Ayler died
'cause his music scared the white man.
Says he used to play like Sonny Rollins
but had to pawn his sax for his longtime love.
Crack.

Sooner give me a poor man
with a little knowledge
than a rich man with an army.
I read mad-avid all the time when I was a kid,
but still ran in and out of backdoors,
splashed in downpours,
screamed at the tv,
sang along to Dekker and Presley,
craved ice cream and curry goat.

Give me the drunkalready over
the sober fool,
the drunkalready singing
'If I had the keys to the world
I'd give you everything.'

A Rancid Poetry

'For two people to live in peace they must both want peace.'
Errico Malatesta

Over 3,000 dead due to hospital infection.
Inadequate sanitation.
Absence of cleaning products.
For every 40 patients there is just one nurse.

Patients placed on beds
that have not been disinfected.
Staff so overworked
they have no time to wash their hands.
(There is no antiseptic soap anyway.)
Hospitals run out of medicines,
gloves, gauze and sheets.
There are never any gloves.

The scanning machines break down.
Basic blood tests are no longer carried out.
The labs are closed.
There are never any gloves,
no catheters, no cleaning tissues.
There are never any gloves.

This is not Aleppo,
this is Athens.
A different kind of war.
€300bn in emergency loans
line the pockets of the rich
and the IMF describes a third of Greeks
as 'at risk of poverty'.

They eat bread at soup kitchens
sleep in shop doorways
as the tourists rollick past.

There are never any gloves.
There are never any gloves.

For poetry to be anything now
it must be as rancid and noisome as the times.

Hedge funders drinking in Alexander's Bar
talk of 'workers having an entitlement culture
based on their existence
not on their ability to work and take risks'.

Bile must stain our every word.

'Based on their existence...'

What were once the natural, the inalienable, the sacred
are now the gifts of states, of spivs and rentiers.

Abdi's Blue Guitar

Abdi has a blue guitar
it's plastic, has broken strings,
found it in a skip.
He carries it for protection,
pitches and reels
along Harlesden High Street,
picking up fag ends,
while carrying his blue guitar.

In Mogadishu TFG military
rammed a rifle up his arse.
In a West End shop doorway
someone poured petrol,
set his legs on fire.
He staggers now,
can of brew in one hand
spilling, still carrying his blue guitar.

All time to come just torment
no rhapsody, no screeching jay
no Dichtung, just pain,
lurching, shitting blood.
'The discord merely magnifies.'
Abdi has a blue guitar
no one ever asks
to hear him play.

Acrostic

At first the thrill outweighs the yearning.
Dulls the sun that shines too bright on an empty day.
Distraction turns to craving.
Itching, like scabies.
Crazed longing for that thing that makes the clock stop.
Time retreating to a space of light at the back of the eyes.
Each time you hate it till you love it, then you nod out.
Death flirts in the glint of the spoon, then dances away with the day.

Another Postcode Warrior Gone Straight on the Numbers

I

These place are all about the management
of space and time,
where you go,
when you go there,
how much time you have
to make a phone call
have a shower
breathe fresh air.

These places are all about
how they decide
when you wake up,
when you unlock,
run, play pool,
drop your laundry
get your meds.

These places are all about
how much control
you can lose
before you string up
or cut up
or blow.

These places, if you blow
you have to blow together,
you have to plan
to take back
space and time,
if only till they bleed it back
again from you.

We started a petition 'cause
the idea of a sit down on the yard
was a step too far for some bad men to take.
And I remember you ran round the wing
trying to find the paper
so you could scrub your name off
before it was handed in to the CO.
You were the top boy.
You led the way
to surrender,
the don gorgon of retreat

II

Parkhurst in '69, the walls were thick with blood and shit.
Sadists on overtime, Frankie Fraser called them,
the screws who queued up to beat and batter
until unconscious, then beat and kick and batter
some more, the lads who took part in the
sit down of 20th October.

Parkhurst in '69, where the screams from the seg
never stopped, and Francis Fraser
was hospitalised for six weeks,
Francis Davidson Fraser, who was deemed mad
for trying to attack the hangman Albert Pierrepoint,
on the morning of Derek Bentley's execution in 1953.

III

Another postcode warrior gone straight on the numbers,
from ghetto VIP to VP without even blinking.
Gangster for life as long as he's Enhanced.
Bought his house with bricks, but he's made of straw.

Candy Flip

Last time I saw you
your face was scabbed,
red sores flecking you
head, neck and hands.

You had your mum's death certificate
torn up in your purse,
in scraps with the tenancy agreement
for the flat you'd lost.

You were sleeping in the subway
next to Paddington Green nick,
trying to light your base pipe
all the time we spoke.

I asked you once what your name was.
You replied with a lie
I said 'no, your real name'
You just lied again.

'You can call me what you want.
You can pay me what you've got.
After all this time on road
there is no 'me' to name.'

Call her candy flip
Call her girlfriend
Call her white horse
Call her yeyo

Call her snowflake
Call her champagne
Call her good girl,
Call her Lois Lane

For all I know you're dead now
but it doesn't feel that way.
Your silhouette, translucent,
at the bus stop, remains.

Citizens of Nowhere

We no longer trade bodies for rum,
no longer hold fathers and daughters and mothers and sons
as middle passage cargo, leg-ironed in filth.
Now fathers and daughters and mothers and sons
come in fishing boats and dinghies,
cling to fake life belts and false hopes
of human rights from those who deem them vermin.

And others come from Kracow, Timisoara and Sofia,
to sleep in parks, under bridges,
rotting barges, 6 to a room.

Scarring their hands and lungs and livers
like Dubliners and Kingstonians
generations before.

An exodus impelled by abjection
to thralldom in warehouses,
building sites and homes.

True citizens of nowhere.
We build your basements
your dream kitchens,
wake from sleeping under church pews,
to mend railways
patch your roofing in the rain.

Fuck your borders
Fuck your walls
Fuck your lines in blood and sand

Learning slow to sing again
in Polish
and in Xasa
in English
in Swahili and Kituba
whispering
'we have been naught, we shall be all.'

Comedians

I was 25,
working,
office cleaning
in Soho.
One job
was for
an agent
in entertainment,
who acted
for alternative
comedians.
One of these,
self-proclaimed
a Marxist,
called in
while I
was working.
He had
A shit.
Didn't flush.
Smirked,
then left.
That day
I learned
that for some
equality
is just
a catchphrase

Eviction Day

A pair of rain-wearied Nikes.
A pink soft toy, muddied.
A teething ring.
A blue and brown sweater.
A bargain store tea-set.
A soaking duvet.
Detritus of a life surrendered,
dumped in a roadside heap
when the locks were changed.

Take only what you can carry.
Pack the year into boxes.
The bailiffs' appointment is fixed.
Go sit with your kids
at the HPU.
We'll sift through the wreckage,
see if there's anything
we can use or sell
from the things you've left behind.

Clean bricks hide dirty money.
We're all Rachman's children now.
Digging out new basements
to bury the homeless deep

Four left foot shoes.
A ballet flat.
A black Adidas.
A workboot.

A kid's slipper.
School text books,
and a Post Office statement.
A bundle of mail.
A hospital letter.

See if the shop has some spare boxes.
Try and borrow a neighbour's van.
Sleep in a park.
Sleep in a car.
Bin-diving for survival.
Under bridges, under bushes,
freezing White Lightning and Lyrica nights.

Clean bricks hide dirty money.
We're all Hoogstraten's children now.
Buy-to-rent, buy off-plan.
Dying for a home.

Games

January '85 we had a damp room on Huskisson Street,
and a 2-bar fire
against air that cut your skin at minus 5.

You chasing, placing the heated foil on my stomach
so that I could feel my skin tense and burn.
Me glaring at the ceiling
wired, champing
while *Berlin* played on cliched repeat,
on the Sansui turntable that scratched and growled,
falling slowly into wreckage.

In the morning you always felt so cold
I'd think you were dead,
a sheet of ice between dermis and epidermis.
I'd try to rub you warm again
then snort more whizz,
kick myself out of bed
go out and score for you.

What kind of love?
What kind of game?

My Man Courtney Was Shit at Maths

My man Courtney was shit at maths.
He could judge the weight of a flap in a newspaper wrap
divvy up quarters and grams in bags
16ths and eight balls by eye and by hand
Q balls, half o's, h bombs, bricks.
My man Courtney was shit at maths.

Knew the thickness of a band
like a Zzap D50.
Knew when to get out and when to get lucky.
Retired at thirty
to a condo in Mo'Bay.
My man Courtney was shit at maths.

Never Again?

'If the body had landed a few metres either side, it would have landed on a busy roundabout or near a row of shops.'

To fall from the sky
while chasing a dream.
To fail in the chase
when the dream is a lie.

Minus 60C,
clinging to the undercarriage of a plane.
A 12-hour flight,
dead or half dead by the time you dropped.

And bodies floating always in the Med,
in the Aegean, in the Channel.
Bodies meeting borders,
bodies meeting barbed wire, teargas, stun grenades.

Aleppo burns.
Homs burns.
Mass graves in Sinjar.
A farmer in Burundi says,
'We are sick of people dying like goats.'

Militarise
Criminalise
Exclude

And we're told,
'We have got to break the business model of the criminal
smugglers.'

And coloured bracelets are 'of course' not triangles,
and we can make 8 year-olds sleep in fields of mud
and nothing ever echoes from the past.
We improvise ghettos
with barbed wire, rifle butts and tv cameras,
and drag children from trailer containers
to hold them in freight sheds.

This is the always-already-ever-convenient European
mea culpa.
Slicing and dicing the universal,
we are close to the edge of that 'never again'
that repeats and repeats
while fat white men who hide money overseas
talk of 'one in, one out' and 'fast track returns',
and place a holding camp
between the words 'human' and 'rights'...

Nights

The dawn Harlesden blue light
leaking through a daub of grey cloud.
You still on your corner from last night,
swaying a little, tired, pinned,
saying, 'I've fuckin' given up asking
if anyone wants business.
I just need a fiver so I can get a rock
then get some sleep'.
Round here the night destroys us.
We careen wounded through the days.

No Cream No Crystal

Pimpled and hollowed-out
and more or less out of it,
trying to swap SIMs,
he's twice dropped the phone.
Supposed to be a burner but he forgets to ditch it.
He's yelling now as the train comes to a stop.
Shouting, 'Fam you need to be at the station
with the fucking bones. No cream no crystal, fam.'
So blatant he'll get nicked within five minutes of leaving the
platform.

The best dealer I ever knew
wore custom-fit Saville Row suits
and ran a sandwich delivery service in the City.
You placed your order and a cycle courier turned up at your work.
Food available whenever you wanted it.

Angie

Oh Angie, you're just skin and bone,
scars and burns and bruises.
Your arms are black and blue and red.
You're dying, and you know it.
Still laughing like a little girl
while life turns you to ashes.

It's the hottest day of the year.
You hide your arms under your baseball jacket
to hide the fag burns that are bleeding
on the hottest day of the year

The dust of a butterfly's wing
colours your arms black and red.
The death foretelling
in the light in your eyes.
Oh Angie, you're just skin and bone.
Life turns you to ashes.

On Lucian Freud's *Two Irishmen in W11*

It seems an apparently simple thing.
The accretion of paint to show
the battered, brick-bruised hands of an Irishman.
Except that the paint is worked so hard,
dragged, heaped, built up
with such detailed ferocity
that its workings manifest
that graft which is in the essence of the hands.

Hands that dug roads
dug foundations
put up houses
pulled down walls.
Captured in oils that
look like knuckles scraped as raw
as that life
lived in the shadow
of the Birmingham Six
and the Guildford Four
the fit ups and the beatings.

Watch your mouth, keep your head down
up on the scaffolding,
looking down on the Wharf.

Sitting now,
well-respected, well-hailed.
In your best suit, at ease, at rest.
Someone worth painting
worth effort.
Worth the looking at.

Prison Pallor

The prison pallor never leaves your skin,
black or brown gone dust-grey,
white skin bleached bone-bright.
Like sees like a thousand yards away.
Way-too-pale and body lurching.
Over-accommodating to passers-by
while trying to maintain that
not-beaten-yet swagger.

Back on road I see the Kid'n Play hi-top fade
is back in fashion with kids who never heard of a cameo cut
or saw that kick-dance routine in House Party,
and there's still a 24/7 party
outside Faisal's barbershop
and too-rare summer days
still have Dennis Brown soundtracks
and I'm still prison-pale.

Caught you on the high street.
Shoulder-bumps and real joy
in seeing you again bro,
but we mumble about 'this'n'that'
and you're standing in the wrong place
wrong time for things to be going well.
From sit-downs in the yard
back to your 'no work, no access to the kids' hell.

And we still have that pallor,
fucked-up spectres drifting always
from one purgatory to another.

Redemption

Redemption – from the Latin redemptionem: a buying back. a deliverance.

Delusional – from the Latin delusion: false belief that is resistant to reason or confrontation with fact.

Some of the things recent Justice Secretaries have believed:
'our prisons will be places of rehabilitation
which give those who have made the wrong choices
opportunities for redemption';
'our justice system will rescue young offenders, and those who
may be on the path to offending, from a life of crime';
'our human rights legislation should better protect the
fundamental freedoms we all cherish.'

Too late all this for the 82 who took their own lives in 2014
the 89 the following year
or the 30,706 who self-harmed in 2015
But still...

Too late for Vikki Thompson
Joanne Latham
Michelle Barnes
Sarah Reed.

Since I came home there have been 8 shootings in my borough
and a 70% cut in youth services.
Maybe prison reform just means
flogging off the real estate
and holding the next generation under HDC.
Still, as that Justice Secretary said,
'there is a treasure, if you can only find it,
in the heart of every man.'
And perhaps we may all get a copy of the King James Bible
signed by the Secretary of State for Justice
left on our blue plastic pillows
in our three'd-up cells
in these 'calm, orderly, purposeful places where we can learn
self-discipline'.

Rescue

'Because of capitalism, because of greed my friends...'
Boris Johnson

Somewhere in here
is the story of how we went
from gun pon waist,
poppin Krystal in the back room,
to glass pipe flaring
in the phone booth 3am
then jacking the phone for change
straight after.

Somewhere in here
is the story of how fifteen
of 17 mates
went from scrambler bikes, Northern Soul
and shoplifting
to fraud, forgery, cocaine
firebombs, Ingram MAC10s
and jail time.

Somewhere in here
are Thatcher's other children, who didn't believe,
but had to live as if we did.
Who thought words like, 'the problem with socialism
is that you eventually run out of other people's money'
were a crock of shit,
but if socialism was dead and buried
we'd live our lives on other peoples' money anyway.

Right now I won't tell that story.
In another life in a blues dance
Johnny Too Bad is playing
and I reach over to you but you shrug me off,
walk home down Stapleton Road alone.
And when The Slickers sing,
'You're gonna run to the rock for rescue there will be no rock'
the 'no rock' might come to sound like that life's happy ending.

Mates

I never made the effort to see enough of you,
but when I was inside, every Wednesday you came.
Our solidarity, our fuck-you sarcasm, I failed to do justice to.
I'm Audhumla searching for salt.
I can't find you now, you've fallen from the earth.

Spaces

Give me the crackhead solidarity
of skuttling adventures
shoplifting Oxford Street,
then huddling over roll-ups
divvying the spoils,
over your white Range Rover'd,
gated, valeted grandiosity.
The all-purpose venality
of the canvas Gucci loafered
with their brown leather trims
trafficked shoeshines
and Dubai Shangri-Las.

The things that you fear round here
are what make me feel safe.
Every eye that clocks you
winks at me.
The passing-car basslines
and air clogged with weed smoke
wall off a city space that isn't yours.
And every blackened Martell miniature
keeps you at bay
one day more, while the CCTV
rotates, voyeuristic and aloof,
overseer of our exiguity.

Steps

She takes his hand
leads him down the steps of the bus,
his legs no taller
than the steps themselves.
Fears he might stumble,
if not this time, the next.
The trick to make him
get up, shrug, step out again.

He always steps clockwise
round the yard, against the flow,
collecting fag butts,
hunting in the flower beds, fire buckets,
sifts the papers, unrolls,
collects the scraps and scoops them
into his pouch, always more falling
than captured, stepping round again.

Swear Down

Swear down...
On the CCTV you can see the cop punch her.
Three times.
In the face.
Hard.
He pulls her hair.
You can see her head bounce
when he throws her to the floor.
March 2014 he gets 150 hours community service.
2015 she's in Holloway.
Sends a card
'Mum, this is just to say Merry Xmas... PS. Get me out of jail.'
11 January 2016 she hangs herself.
Sarah Reed. Dead at 32.

Swear down...
He's just sitting talking in the Audi.
Culcheth, Cheshire.
Then the windscreen goes in.
He's shot in the chest.
Dead. Single shot from a Heckler and Koch.
At the public inquiry they try to smear him.
Criminal lifestyle.
Perceived threat.
The QC for the cop who killed him says to his friend
(the friend sitting next to him when his lungs were blown out
through his back)
'You were going to commit armed robbery weren't you?'
'You'd have to be armed to commit armed robbery wouldn't
you?' he replies.
Anthony Grainger. 3 March 2012. Unarmed. Killed by cops.
Aged 36.

Swear down...
In his photograph
he looks younger than he is.
Baby-faced
with a Burberry check scarf.
Just a kid really.
But a father too.
They chased him into a 24/7 shop.
You can see the cop push him to the ground
hold him down by the neck
and stick his fingers
into his mouth, down his throat, choking him.
His next-door neighbour said,
'Some people are handed a silver platter in life, and some
people are handed a pile of shit'.
Rashan Charles. Twenty years old. Father of Remiya.
Died 22 July 2017.

Swear down...

The Beautiful Boys and Girls

The beautiful boys and girls of Liverpool '81 are dying.
The fat and balding also-rans.
Broken-backed.
Opiated.
Pissed.
Jailed.
Gouching.
Stiffed.

The beautiful boys and girls of Liverpool '81 are losers.
What were we fighting for, those days
when Upper Parly Street was fogged with CS gas
and David Moore was murdered?
The right to not be slammed against red-brick walls
by cops with bitter-stale breath who spittle-sneered
and called us faggots?
The right to dress like New York dolls in a city
crazed, outraged by
teenage boys in leather kecks?
We wanted speed and vapor trails and dub-wild nights
at Stanley House, the Somali and the Casa.
Guitars and drugs and home-made clothes
would change the world.
And we'd go gary'd up to Kirklands

And oh what a mess we made.
As we fell apart.
And nothing changed.
And we rarely speak.
And our slaveport city
remains a racist cesspit.

And now we've lost you. You were
the sashaying best and worst of all of us.
So we'll raise a glass to the peacock glory
of your domino days.
Now all that's left
of all we tried to be
are monochrome prints
on Facebook pages.

The Best of Society

Some causes of ill-health
within my friends and family group
From '48 to date:

Pneumonoconiosis
Angina
Depression
Metastasised bowel cancer
Motor neurone disease
Dementia
Ischemic heart disease
HIV/AIDS
Systemic lupus
Peripheral neuropathy.

We are meat giving way
to disease and decay
with the NHS in place
to catch us, patch us up.
Alleviate the worst
of poverty and work
as we tumble to our graves.

The Pilipino nurse who washed and shaved my father.
The Egyptian surgeon who told us he'd done all he could.
The St Marys epidemiologists
who improvised welfare rights and housing advice
for rent boys sleeping night-sweat rough in Rupert Street.
An underpaid polyglot army of care.
Showing the best of society while society's erased.

The envy of the world.
Praised by every hat in the ring.
While the engineering
of austerity
hacks open the wounds of a different kind of crisis
in a bloody, operose war.

The Exact Reverse is True

Ladbroke Grove used to have a Dub Vendor store
at number 150. Now that shop sells mobile phones.
I can remember some of the vinyl I bought from there.
A Delroy Wilson album with *Better Must Come*.
Michael Prophet's *Gunman*
Wayne Smith, Tenor Saw
(*Victory Train* on a twelve alongside all his big tunes on pre)
All the Jammys and Taxi and George Phang tunes
that soundtracked my twenties.

And *Murderer*.
Murderer by Buju Banton.
Murderer by Barrington Levy.
The Buju tune goes
'Murderer
Blood is on your shoulders
Kill I today you cannot kill I tomorrow'.

There are 'Missing' posters plastered all round Ladbroke Grove.
The faces of the missing who are the not-yet-officially-dead
of Grenfell Tower, which stands now
a 24-storey fire-black column
sucking all the light out of this year's spring,
and shadowing the Grove.

Not far from here Aswad recorded *Live and Direct*
Meanwhile Gardens, Carnival, 1982.
Horns callin' down Jah fire and bassline thunder
and Brinsley Forde yelling 'Murderah'
and the crowd all ravin' and shoutin' 'Murderah'.
But no-one's ravin' now.

*'The £10m building refurbishment included the installation of
insulated exterior cladding, new double-glazed windows and a new
communal heating system.'*

Mothers throwing babies from windows.
Mothers throwing babies from windows.

*The two-year project, which was designed and delivered by
KCTMO in partnership with Rydon Construction, was a complex
one as it took place with all 120 flats occupied throughout. The
logistics had to be carefully managed to minimise disruption.'*

Mothers throwing babies from windows.
The windows all blown out now.
You can still see shreds of curtains
and the patterns on some – a horse, an owl.
Cauterised, flapping.

At the next meeting
of the full council at K&C
shout 'Murderah, murderah'
till all of them reach jail.

*'The opponents of so-called austerity seek to paint the supporters
of sound finances as selfish or uncaring. The exact reverse is true.'*

We are the ungrateful bastard brothers and sisters
of the burned-alive,
selfishly shouting 'murderah , murderah, murderah'.

Another tune I remember buying at Dub Vendor,
Johnny Osbourne *Thirteen Dead, Nothing Said*.
That one was produced by Aswad.
And the Linton Kwesi Johnson album
Making History
with the track *New Cross Massakeh*.
John La Rose called the New Cross fire
'an unparalleled act of barbaric violence
against the black community.'

I guess history teaches us to be wary
of words like 'unparalleled.'

The Victors are Always Victors

The victors are always victors
because we have allowed them
to forget what it is like to lose.

I have a pond in the garden
however much it leaks,
I always forget I have to fill it.
Animal skulls when I turn the soil.
Burn blast bones in the soils on Highway 80
Gum tree
Jericho Rose
Red Yucca.

The act of remembering
can be an act of revolt.

The victors because we have
are always victors.
Allowed them what it is like
to forget to lose.

What it is like
are always
forget to lose
victors.

Victors
forget to lose.

Forget
Victors
Lose.

To Hell with Property

Clean look, contrasting
empathetic companion colours,
complementary whites,
eggshell exterior midsheen.
All our paint is eco-friendly,
low odour and child safe.
Off white.
Old white.
Sudbury yellow.
The headlong avidity of buy-to-let.

Someone's put an old sofa out.
There's a sleeping bag on it.
Go past early enough
you'll see a pile of blankets
left behind by the Romanian plasterer
who's made it his home.

Top Shotta

From '72, top PNP shotta,
in defence of equal pay and free education
while the CIA armed Lester Coke
at Tivoli Gardens.
You wore a bullet round your neck
as a fetish, like Manley's Kariba suit.

When Seaga won in '80 you moved to SW9.
Better never come.
Cold winters and cold flats.
The bullet replaced
by Cherry B bottles and overproof miniatures.
Lined up to repel the days.

Life Sentence

after Aram Saroyan

A life sentence.

William Burroughs on Brownlow Hill

I once saw William Burroughs
in a newsagent on Brownlow Hill.
Looked like a turtle in a gabardine mac.
Bowed by the whipping Irish wind
but calm as death or Kansas.

Autumnal

Autumn in the air already
the softening and lowering
of the light.
Another year wasted.
The littered days.

The Ronnie Spector of Shiel Road

You always looked as cool as fuck.
Black hair, black leathers, black shades.
Always leaning against the same wall
day and night on Shiel Road.
An ice sculpture of Ronnie Spector,
melting in the sometime sunlight.

At school you used to
rip pages out of poetry books
and stick them on your bedroom wall
next to the Bowie poster
and the Runaways sleeve
you'd pinned there.

No-one else had Baudelaire wallpaper
with a Wreck of the Deutschland stripe
and Mallarmé stars.
Now you say 'I've written another poem.
Will suck cock for rock.'
We both laugh.
But we know it's not funny.
Not really.

Met your mum again.
Me and her at your funeral.
And it didn't rain.
She said at one time
you used to try to make every sentence sing,
just like Ronnie Spector.

I told her you'd never stopped.
Black hair, black leathers, black shades.
Always leaning against the same wall
day and night on Shiel Road.
A glass statue of infinite cool,
stress cracks showing in the nightlight.

No other crackhead
could recite Verlaine from memory.
Life never plays out how you think it should.
You thought there were diamonds on Shiel Road
but it was silicon carbide in the streetglow.
Nothing funny in that joke now.
Not really.

Mystery Trains

There's a train a comin.

Curtis Mayfield. Key of F. Curtis, the Muddy Waters fan from Cabrini Green whose songs were the hopeful gospel call-out for the Freedom Rides. Curtis Mayfield in '65. The same year Malcolm X (who said 'Every defeat contains its own seed...') was shot dead at the Audobon Ballroom.

We were talking today about the decline in the use of the train as musical metaphor, capturing all that gets caught up in the possibility of accidental encounters and fresh starts. The joyful thunder of Take the A-Train. The snarling judgement-call of *Slow Train Coming*. The Beastie Boys jumpin the turnstyle, groggy-eyed and fried on *Stop That Train*.

Now no one buys a ticket to ride. It's just ride-outs to opp-blocks, with Rambos and waps, and you can't hear the rhythm of the freight train passing for the ching ching ching and the blade hitting bone and the doors of our cells clanging shut.

Except there's a girl on the Bakerloo Line with her mates, carrying cardboard signs that say Silence = Violence, journeyin' with all the stellar righteousness of youth. And La Bestia is pulling into Platform Two, carrying unillusioned reinforcements.

People get ready.

In memoriam

an un-named suicide, Willesden Junction, 1892

There is a before
but no after.

What drew you here?
Debt or mourning?
A marriage turned to kicks, cut lips,
cracked teeth and bruises.
Knitting needles, hot baths, gin,
bleach, deeper cuts, more bruises.

Passengers on station steps
crossing, changing, coming-together.
Routes, rails, somewhere else to go.
That looking forward, moving on,
you left behind.

How long it took, how swift or slow?
One night, one life passing.
In this place of convergence.
An ending...

Drug War Poems

after Adrian Henri

1. Sixteen and seventeen year olds from San Salvador, Guatamala City, Tegucigalpa. At the US/Mexico border. Hanging on the wire. Super mano dura.

2. Dead hand holds a poppy in Musa Qala as the B-52s pass overhead.

3. Feltham A/ stink of shit / *'40% of children said they had felt unsafe at some point during their stay'*/ shank the cunt/ where you from/ do him at unlock/ OVER THE TOP/ Children/ They are/Just fuckin children/ *'As a result, 'keep apart' policies – developed so that children from rival gangs, or who for other reasons are likely to be violent to each other, are kept separate – have come to dominate'.* / Never had a visit/ Sent me a letter but I couldn't fuckin read it/Smoke this bro/ Look at him/Like a fish floppin about/Prick/ *'This has led to a collapse of any reasonable regime, prevented many children from getting to education or training, delayed their access to health care, isolated them from meaningful human interaction and frustrated them to the point where violence and self-harm have become the means to express themselves or gain attention.'*/ Was it for this the clay grew tall?

4. Which side were you on in the Drug Whore ?

5. Trap house quiet. Playin X-box. The jaded dead.

6. Owen and Spender swappin rhymes at a wake in Lewisham for some kid who got off the P4 to meet his girl in Brixton McDonalds. I call my man 'son', 'cause he shines like/ move him into the/ Sun

7. Quayside to quayside in Gucci loafers. Columbia to Mexico. Cargo crates at the port in Malaga. Just a small villa outside Puerto Banus.

8. Don't be vague. Blame... Nixon? Reagan? Clinton? Thatcher? Blair? Cameron?

9. There is no armistice. No amnesty. No white feathers because there is no choice. There is poverty in Baltimore and Brent and there is cocaine in the cubicles of Parliament. We could wear white poppies but there's no Remembrance Day.

10. 2016 / 2,593 registered deaths in England and Wales related to drug misuse / funeral barges heaped with skulls floating out to a termagant sea.

Hawks

A surpassing stillness.
You're impalpable
in the 7am tumult
and your cold, tractable,
gaze sweeps across
the bus-stop loiterers,
cashpoint shufflers,
homebound indentured grafters,
until someone
lets a fag-butt drop
and you swoop.
It's still lit
so you draw deep,
exhale,
then take up your post again.

No one round here
drops fivers any more,
not even a pound coin.
I saw a 20p piece
a few weeks ago,
silver flashing
in a dried-out gully bed

You've taken on some of the properties
of a hawk.
Surveying your tapped-out, barren field.
Plummeting, careening, then scurrying for change.

Alive

You look like Anita Pallenberg in '65
if Anita Pallenberg was being eaten alive from the inside.
Cheekbones you're dying for
blistered lips, mouth full of choked up black shit,
dancing on the broken glass under the dawning stars
in the places the cameras don't reach.

So we party hard
still raving in the daylight,
catching the lamplit morning
but not the morning's dread.
Dreads flashing locks, unwavering.
We follow the bass pulse from shebeen
to crackhouse, high-stepping,
ecstatic, galled, psychotic.
Refusing to flinch
while being buried alive.

Abraded, abjected, degraded.
Sanctioned, dismantled, unmade.
Playing Russian Roulette
with a glass pipe
staying high to pretend
to stay alive.

I Used to be Somebody Else

Slept right through.
Woke up this morning.
But still midnight.
Midnight in the century.
And it never fucking ends.

They'd privatise the air.
They'd privatise the air.
They'd privatise the fucking air.

I used to be somebody else.
Dead Russians told me words were weapons.
But weapons make better weapons than words.

Read in the paper
A man beat a puppy to death
with a hammer.
Fucking cunt.

If the puppy had been named
Hope or Possibility
maybe that would have formed
the basis for an analogy.
But he'd still be a fuckin cunt.

It ought to be possible to outthink the prison of class and if not
outthink it then batter it out of existence with the force of spite
and misery that makes your muscles and bones ache when you
find the dole payment is late and you have no food money and
can't even afford a can of fucking lager and the bailiffs write and
say they will be calling tomorrow to remove the goods you don't
have and you wait till they come round and tell them if you can
find something worth takin you're welcome to fuckin try and
the room feels even smaller and this life is just a fucking
lockdown and the key to unlock it is money and you never have
any and you never fuckin will.

I used to be somebody else.

Counted 11 homeless crammed into doorways, holding onto
their cardboard life rafts, on The Broadway today. One just
swaddled and asleep in the middle of the pavement as if he
could obstruct the flow of disinterest just by being there,
disconsolate and passive.

I used to be somebody else.

But I can cook up rock
I can boost your Porsche
I can trick your name
I can pass through walls.

Been a roadsman
Dirtsman
Beggarman
Thief,
but never snitched
never sold-out.
Watched plenty men
turn and flip
and tout.

I used to be somebody else.
Maybe bliss is just
strong lager and a big dog for company
and if you're lucky
somewhere quiet to doss down.
Kenny is pissing against the bus stop
pants round his ankles.
It's daylight.
Midnight across 2 centuries.
He's shouting about
fucking wolves
have eaten his legs
and he's headbutting the bus-stop window

'Fuckin wolves, man
Fuckin wolves!'
Is it better to think
you're being eaten by wolves
in your dreams
than to know the wolves have already
taken everything round here
down to the bones
and moved on?

I used to be somebody else

Kensal Green cemetery.
Queen of the Meadow and purple dead-nettles.
Graves wracked and buckled and cracked
by swelling London clay.
I watch the Holly Blues and Orange Tips flicker and swarm.
I used to be somebody else.
Turning slowly now
to nobody at all.

Notes

Prisoner Information Service
As of July 2021, the UK prison population stood at 78,488 hells.

PSI 30/2013
This was the Prison Service instruction which sets out the Incentives and Earned Privileges scheme, used by Minister for Justice Chris Grayling to limit prisoners' access to books.

Racaille
Nicolas Sarkozy refereed to rioters as 'racaille' (scum) when he called for them to be cleared from the streets with high pressure hoses.

The Exact Reverse is True
The first two quotations are taken from a Kensington and Chelsea Tenant Management Organisation press release, 13 May 2016, celebrating the refurbishment of Grenfell Tower. The third is by George Osborne.

Acknowledgements

Thanks to the editors of the following publications, in which versions of some of these poems have previously appeared: *Koestler Voices, Proletarian Poetry, Magma, New River Press* and *Poets for Grenfell.*

Over the years, the following told me to get my head out of my arse and focus on my writing, so thanks to Ross Reid, Dave McCullough, Jackie Leven (RIP), Pete Fulwell (RIP), Roger Hill, Pete Wylie (A Word To the Wise Guy still nails best what was done to our class in the 80s, 'only torture for the likes of us...'), Massey Clark, Stephen Shaw, Keith Hassell, Helen Ward, Maggie Harley, Pat Hayes, Gail Lewis. I got there eventually...

Thank you to the families of the 96, Anthony Grainger and Mark Duggan for refusing to just swallow the shit that's given to them.

Thanks to David Dunkley, Alex and Lorraine Hamilton-Clarke, the Piersons, and others (you know who you are) for their support while inside. Thanks to Ian, Phil, Pete, Bharat, Farrukh, Rocky, Junior, Reddz, Lyrics, Biggs, Norman, Paddy, Little Paul, the other Moss, Steve, Charlie and the Postie for all the laughs on the landings. Thanks to Fred Fillingham, Bob Knapp, Frank Smith. Donald Brown RIP. Michael Tyrell RIP.

Thanks to the Koestler Trust, Esmée Fairbairn Foundation, and the Society for Authors for their support.

Thanks to Kate Davey for her encouragement. Thanks to the Willesden Junction Poets. Thanks to Miriam Nash for being a wonderful mentor and friend.

Kevin Lane-INNOCENT!   Michael Stone-INNOCENT!
3 the guys.

Thanks, with all my love, to Mum, and to my wife Stephanie O'Brien, for being there, seeing this through and for everything, really.